D1503226

VISITING MEXICO

SOUTH OF THE BORDER

Laura Conlon

The Rourke Book Company, Inc.
Vero Beach, Florida 32964

© 1994 The Rourke Book Company, Inc.

Edited by Sandra A. Robinson

PHOTO CREDITS
© Frank Balthis: cover, pages 4, 12; © James P. Rowan: pages
7, 13; © Jerry Hennen: page 15; © Fred Lyon: page 18; courtesy
Mexico's Ministry of Tourism: title page (Blake Discher), pages 8
(Blake Discher), 10, 17, 21

Library of Congress Cataloging-in-Publication Data

Conlon, Laura, 1959-
    Visiting Mexico / by Laura Conlon.
        p.   cm. — (South of the border)
    ISBN 1-55916-057-8
    1. Mexico—Description and travel—Juvenile literature. I. Title.
II. Series.
F1210.C668   1994
917.204'835—dc20   94-11189
                                                          CIP
                                                          AC

Printed in the USA

TABLE OF CONTENTS

VISITING MEXICO

Tourists, or visitors, to Mexico find many things to do and see. Tourists enjoy the beautiful landscapes of the country — the mountains, seashores and forests. They enjoy seeing life in country villages, which are the same today as they were hundreds of years ago.

Many people visit the **ruins** of the mighty Indian civilizations of long ago.

Mexican festivals, sports, music and dance are exciting for tourists, too.

Tourists can ride in small boats among gray whales that winter in the warm seas off Baja California

RESORTS

People from all over the world come to Mexico's beautiful **resorts.** Resorts are places where people often go for vacation.

The Pacific Coast cities of Acapulco and Puerto Vallarta are known for their beautiful beaches, luxury hotels, and warm, sunny weather.

The islands of Cancun and Cozumel off the Gulf of Mexico are popular resorts, too.

A tourist strolls along the beach at Cancun, Mexico

RUINS

Long ago, ancient Indians lived in the lands that today are part of Mexico. These ancient people included the Olmec, the Maya, the Toltec and the Aztec Indians.

Each tribe built beautiful cities and created wonderful statues and art. The remains, or ruins, left by these people still exist today. Visitors can see these ruins, and learn much about the lives of these ancient people. One of the world's tallest pyramids is in the ruins of the city, Teotihuacan (tay oh tee wah KAHN).

Tourists visit the ruins of the ancient Mayan civilization at Chichén Itzá

MEXICO CITY

Mexico City is one of the two largest cities in the world, with nearly 20 million people. It is the capital of Mexico, and it is the oldest city in North America. Mexico City is home to many monuments, amazing ancient ruins, and museums filled with art and treasures from long ago.

Life in Mexico City is much like life in a large city in the United States or Canada. There are gleaming skyscrapers and busy streets. Mexico City has one of the best **subways** in the world.

Mexico City's works of art, monuments and ancient ruins attract thousands of tourists

Tourists begin a hike on Cedros Island off the Baja Peninsula

Tulum National Park on the Yucatan Peninsula lures visitors with white sand, clear seas and ancient ruins

MEXICO'S VILLAGES

To reach some of the very **remote** villages in Mexico, people have to ride horses or burros, also called donkeys. Life in many small farming villages has been the same for hundreds of years.

People often farm by hand, or with the help of oxen. Everyone in the family, even the small children, help with farming.

Some Mexican farmers live in houses made of **adobe,** or sun-dried bricks. Often the floors are dirt.

Adobe buildings and burros, or donkeys, are still common in Mexican villages.

THE MARKETS

In large cities or small villages, the market is an important part of Mexican life. In some places, market day is the highlight of the week, and people come from all over to shop and visit.

People gather in the town plaza for a market day. There they find small stands filled with fruits and vegetables, T-shirts, jewelry and just about anything you can imagine. Later in the day, people often take part in *paseos,* or evening walks around the plaza.

A Mexican boy gathers daisies to sell at a village market

SPORTS

Visitors to Mexico can enjoy several sports. Soccer is the leading sport. The beautiful Azteca Stadium in Mexico City fills with fans for every game.

The Spanish settlers brought bullfighting to Mexico. Crowds cheer "Ole!" as the brave **matador,** or bullfighter, fights the angry bull. The Plaza de Toros Monumental in Mexico City is the world's largest bullfighting ring.

Visitors can also see a Mexican-style rodeo called a *charreada.* Horsemen show off skillful riding and roping.

Bullfighting is a popular sport in Mexico

FIESTAS AND FESTIVALS

Mexicans celebrate many holidays with **fiestas,** or parties. Fiestas are usually filled with music, dancing and fireworks.

Many fiestas honor religious days. Christmas fiestas last nine days. On All Souls Day — November 2 — Mexicans leave out food for the dead, who they believe return once a year.

Saints' Days are special festivals honoring the many saints. Guadelupe Day — December 12 — is one of the most important.

Bright costumes and dancing highlight Mexican festivals

THE PLAZA OF THREE CULTURES

La Plaza de Tres Culturas, "The Plaza of Three Cultures," is a good place to learn about Mexico's past and present. This **plaza** is in Mexico City. It is made up of buildings from each of the three **cultures,** or ways of life, in Mexico — Indian, Spanish and modern Mexican.

The ruins of an **ancient** Indian pyramid stand at one end of the plaza. Nearby is an old church built by the Spanish, who ruled Mexico for 300 years. A modern glass and steel building is also in the plaza.

Glossary

adobe (ah DOH bee) — bricks made of clay and dried in the sun

ancient (AIN chent) — very old

culture (KULT cher) — a group of people's way of life

fiesta (fee ESS tah) — the Spanish world for "feast" or "festival"; any kind of party

matador (MAT a door) — a bullfighter

plaza (PLAH zah) — a public square, usually in the center of town, where the main buildings are located

remote (re MOTE) — far away or out-of-the-way

resort (re ZORT) — a place where people often go for vacation

ruins (ROO inz) — the remains of a fallen building or city

subway (SUB way) — an underground railway

tourist (TOOR ist) — a person who takes a trip to learn more about a place

INDEX